Haruna's Story Part 1

I Talk You Talk Press

Copyright © 2018 I Talk You Talk Press

ISBN: 978-4-909733-09-2

www.italkyoutalk.com

info@italkyoutalk.com

Image copyright: Woman: © naka #35189354 Standard License
Cosmetics: © Mrkvica #32735013 Standard License

CONTENTS

IMPORTANT!

In this story, there are some Japanese words.
The Japanese words are
1. *shacho* - Company President/CEO
2. *kacho* - section manager
3. *san* - Mr/Ms (E.g. Tanaka san = Mr Tanaka)
4. *sensei* - teacher

INTRODUCTION

Nice Ume-leaf Cosmetics is a very famous cosmetics company in Japan. The quality of the products is very high. The company sells cosmetics in all the large department stores in Japan. The president, Takahashi shacho, wants to start selling the cosmetics in other countries. He wants to open a shop in the USA, so the staff at Nice Ume-leaf Cosmetics must learn to speak English.

Haruna Yamane is from Shimane, Japan. She is twenty-seven. She works for Nice Ume-leaf Cosmetics in Tokyo. She likes her job very much. She moved to Tokyo from Shimane when she was eighteen years old. After she graduated from university, she started working in the cosmetics company. She likes cosmetics and fashion very much.

Kana Matsumoto is from Tokyo. She is thirty. She is Haruna's co-worker. She wants to be a manager in the company in the future. She works very hard. Kana usually works on Saturdays and Sundays too. She often stays at work until 11:00pm.

CHAPTER ONE

It is 7:30am on Monday morning. Haruna is on the train. She is going to work. There are many people on the train, so she cannot sit down. She has to stand up. It takes one hour to get to her office by train.

She arrives at her office at 8:30.

"Good morning Tanaka kacho," she says to her office manager, Mr Tanaka.

"Good morning. Oh, Yamane san, we are going to have a meeting at 9:00am. It is a very important meeting," says Tanaka kacho.

"Yes, Tanaka kacho," says Haruna. "I understand."

Haruna sits at her desk and switches on her computer.

"Good morning!" Her co-workers start to arrive.

"Oh, good morning Matsumoto san," says Haruna.

Kana Matsumoto is Haruna's co-worker. She is a strong woman and she works very hard.

"Matsumoto san, we have a meeting at 9:00 this morning. Tanaka kacho said it is an important meeting," says Haruna.

"Yes, I know. Tanaka kacho told me on Friday night."

"On Friday night?"

"Yes. You went home at 7:00pm on Friday. But I worked until 11:00pm with Tanaka kacho. He told me about the meeting then."

"Oh, I see," says Haruna. *Kana always works so hard. I must work harder like Kana,* thinks Haruna.

It is 9:00am. Everyone is sitting in the meeting room.

"Good morning everyone," says Tanaka kacho.

"Good morning Tanaka kacho."

"I have an important announcement to make," says Tanaka kacho. "Our company makes very good cosmetic products. Japanese women like our products very much. The president, Takahashi shacho, thinks that women in other countries will also like our products. So, he wants to open Nice Ume-leaf Cosmetics shops in other countries."

"That's a great idea!" says Kana.

"Yes, I think so too," says Tanaka kacho. "However, your jobs will change."

"Change?" says Haruna.

"Yes. Now, we are a Japanese brand. But Takahashi shacho wants to create an international brand. He wants our cosmetics to be famous and popular around the world. So, everyone in this office must learn to speak English."

"I love English!" says Kana.

"And, you must all get 700 points on the TOEIC test this year."

"700 points?!" says Haruna.

"Yes. 700 points. The first new shop will be in New York. It will open next year. Before then, you must all get 700 on the TOEIC test."

"What happens if we don't get 700?" asks Haruna.

"If you don't get 700, you will lose your jobs," says Tanaka kacho. Everyone is shocked.

"And, the person who gets the highest score can go to our new shop in the USA, and work there for a year," says Tanaka kacho.

Haruna is excited. When she was young, her dream was to work abroad. She would like to work abroad for a year.

"Who would like to work in the USA?" asks Tanaka kacho.

"I would like to work abroad!" says Kana.

"I would like to work abroad too!" says Haruna.

The other workers don't want to work abroad. Only Kana and Haruna want to work abroad.

"OK. Everyone in this office must get 700 points. Yamane san and Matsumoto san, the person with the highest score can work in the USA."

Haruna looks at Kana. Kana is smiling.

"I love English. I have friends from the USA. They will help me to study," says Kana.

Haruna feels nervous. She has no friends from the USA, and she does not study English.

"When is the TOEIC test?" asks Haruna.

"July," says Tanaka kacho.

"July?" asks Haruna. "That is very soon."

"Yes, it is. It is April now, so you have three months to study," says Tanaka kacho.

The meeting finishes. Everyone returns to their desk and starts working.

"Yamane san, have you ever taken TOEIC before?" asks Kana.

"No, I haven't. Have you?" asks Haruna.

"Yes, I have. I took it three years ago."

"What was your score?" asks Haruna.

Kana laughs. "That's a secret!"

I wish I had studied English more in school, thinks Haruna.

When Haruna was at junior high school, she loved English. But when she went to high school, she didn't like English. There were too many tests. She wanted to speak English, but her teacher only taught grammar and reading. It was very boring. She wanted to go abroad on a working holiday, but her father said 'no'. Her father told her to go to a Japanese university, and then get a good job in a Japanese company. So, she gave up on her dream. Now, she has a chance to work in the USA for a year. But now, she has to start studying English hard.

"Matsumoto san, where do you study English?" Haruna asks Kana.

"That is also a secret, Yamane san! You want to work in the shop in the USA, and I want to work in the shop in the USA too. You are my rival!" says Kana.

CHAPTER TWO

At lunchtime, Haruna usually goes to a restaurant near her office. But today, she buys a rice ball and eats it outside the convenience store. Then, she goes to a bookshop.

Haruna looks at the books on the bookshelf. TOIEC Starter...TOEIC 400...TOEIC 500...TOEIC 600...TOEIC 700...She picks up the TOEIC 700 book and opens it. She looks at the first page. There are so many long words! She closes the book quickly. She picks up the TOEIC 400 book and looks at the first few pages. She understands some of the words, but the book looks like her high school English textbook. She has bad memories of her high school English textbook.

Haruna looks at the price on the back of the book. 2,000 yen. It is expensive, but she has to get a TOEIC score of 700 in July. She decides to buy all of the books from TOEIC Starter to TOEIC 700. She pays 10,000 yen. It is very expensive, but Haruna must study.

Haruna gets home from work at 7:00pm. It takes one hour to get from her office to her small apartment by train. She is very tired. She wants to watch TV and relax with a glass of wine, but she has to study English. She eats rice and vegetables for dinner, and then takes a bath. Then, at 8:30pm, she sits at the dining room table and opens her textbooks. She starts to study.

By 11:30pm she is very tired. She has studied for three hours. She has written all the new vocabulary in a notebook. Tomorrow morning, she will study the words in her notebook on the train. She goes to bed and falls asleep very quickly.

The next day, Haruna goes to work. She feels very tired. She works very hard. At 11:00am, she starts to feel sleepy. She decides to take a break. She goes to the office kitchen and makes a cup of coffee. She opens her notebook.

Kana walks into the kitchen. She looks at Haruna.

"What is that?" asks Kana.

"It's my English notebook," says Haruna. "I studied these words last night."

Kana looks at the vocabulary in Haruna's notebook.

"Express train…platform…ticket…these words are easy Yamane san! Very easy!"

Haruna feels sad. She must study harder.

CHAPTER THREE

It is May.

Haruna has been studying English for a month. She has finished TOIEC Starter and TOEIC 400. Her notebook is full of new vocabulary and phrases. But she is very tired, and she forgets the words easily.

One day, she arrives home and opens her mail box. There is a pamphlet for an English conversation school in her mailbox. She looks at the pamphlet.

English conversation classes! Group classes! Private classes! Enjoy studying with Jake sensei from the USA! Come to our school and take a free trial lesson! We will help you!! Yes We Can!!

There are only two months left until the TOEIC test. Haruna decides to go to the English school on Sunday afternoon to get more information.

On Sunday, Haruna walks into the school. There is an office and a classroom.

An American man meets Haruna in the lobby. He is very tall, and has short brown hair, and a friendly smile.

"Hi! I'm Jake. Nice to meet you," says the American teacher.

"Er...hello...I'm Haruna...nice to meet you, too," says Haruna. She is nervous because she hasn't spoken English for a long time.

"So, why do you want to study English, Haruna?" asks Jake.

"Er...because...I need to get...700 on the TOEIC test."

"The TOEIC test? OK. When is your test?"

"July."

"How long have you been studying English?"

"Only for a month. I use TOEIC textbooks, but I forget the words easily."

"I see. If you don't use the words in conversation, you will forget them easily. I think you should come here for classes. In my conversation classes, you can use the words you learn in your textbook. You need speaking practice," says Jake.

"How much are classes?"

"Group classes are 2,000 yen per hour, and private classes are 10,000 yen per hour," says Jake.

"10,000 yen?! That's too expensive for me!" says Haruna.

"Okay, so how about the group class?" asks Jake.

"How many students are in the class?" asks Haruna.

"There are three students in the middle level class. That class is on Monday nights. There are eight students in the beginner class. That class is on Tuesday nights."

"Eight students? That's too many!" says Haruna.

"OK, why don't you come for a trial lesson on Monday night?" asks Jake.

"Yes, OK, I will do that," says Haruna.

"See you then!" says Jake.

"Bye!" says Haruna. She walks out of the school. *I am going to start English lessons! Jake sensei will help me! I can get 700 points on the TOEIC test!* she thinks.

It is Monday night. Haruna is nervous. She arrives at the English school. She walks into the classroom. There are three students in the classroom.

"Hi Haruna! Come in! Sit down!" says Jake.

"Oh! Yamane san!" shouts one of the students.

Haruna looks at her. "Oh, Matsumoto san!" Haruna is very shocked. Kana is a student in the class!

"Yamane san, are you going to join this class?" asks Kana.

"I don't know yet," says Haruna.

"Well, this class is very high level. I think you should join the beginner class on Tuesdays," says Kana.

Haruna sits down. Kana is always saying bad things. Haruna does not like her, and she does not want to study in the same class as Kana.

The lesson starts.

"OK everyone, today we have a trial student – Haruna Yamane. Haruna, please introduce yourself," says Jake.

Haruna stands up.

"Er, hi. My name is Haruna Yamane. I am from Shimane," says Haruna.

"Where is Shimane?" asks Jake.

"Er…it's in..er….nishi". Haruna stops. Nishi…what is 'nishi' in English…

"It is in western Japan," says Kana.

"Oh, I see," says Jake. "Thank you Kana."

"Yamane san, nishi is 'west' in English," says Kana. "Did you forget?"

Haruna sits down. She wants to go home. In the lesson, the other students talk a lot. Haruna wants to speak, but the other students are talking very fast. She cannot join the conversation. She sits quietly and waits for the class to finish.

Haruna decides not to join the English school. She does not want to study with Kana. Also, the lower level class has too many students, and private classes are too expensive. She will use her textbooks and study harder.

CHAPTER FOUR

It is Friday, July 1st, the day of the TOEIC test. Haruna tries her best, but the test is difficult for her. She couldn't answer some of the questions and she couldn't understand the listening questions. The listening conversations were so fast!

She hears Kana talking to Adachi san, one of her co-workers.

"Adachi san, how was the test?" asks Kana.

"It was very difficult. I couldn't answer many of the questions. How about you Matsumoto san?" asks Mr. Adachi.

"Well, some questions were difficult, but some questions were easy," says Kana. "The listening was very easy for me, because I study with an American teacher, and I have many friends from other countries," says Kana.

Haruna feels even sadder. *Maybe I should give up my dream…Kana is so much better than me at speaking English….Tanaka kacho will send Kana to the USA,* she thinks.

Then, she remembers Tanaka kacho's words -"If you don't get 700, you will lose your jobs."

I have to get a score of 700! If I don't, I will lose my job! thinks Haruna. Haruna goes home feeling very stressed.

Haruna will get her TOEIC test results next week. Did she get 700? Did she get a higher score than Kana?

CHAPTER FIVE

(A week later)

Tanaka kacho walks into the office.

"Everyone, please come to the meeting room now. We are going to have a meeting about your TOEIC scores," he says. He does not look happy. Haruna and her co-workers are very nervous.

Everyone walks into the meeting room and sits down.

"I will announce your TOIEC scores. Adachi san – 450, Sato san – 540, Saito san – 580, Matsumoto san – 650, Yamane san – 585."

Haruna is very shocked.

585! That is too low! But no-one got 700...so will we all lose our jobs? thinks Haruna.

She looks at Kana. Kana looks very angry. *Even Kana didn't get 700, and she has been studying English with Jake for a long time. What will Tanaka kacho say?*

"Everyone tried their best on the test, but no one got 700," says Tanaka kacho.

"I spoke to Takahashi shacho about your scores. He decided to give you a second chance. Maybe three months was too short to study and get 700. So, you have another chance."

"When is the test?" asks Kana.

"It is in January," says Tanaka kacho. "You have six months to study. Please study hard. Do you have any questions?"

"Is the test in January our last chance?" asks Haruna.

"Of course. It is your last chance," says Tanaka kacho.

It is Friday evening. Haruna is studying. She feels very tired. She worked until 9:00pm. Then, she bought cup noodles from the convenience store for dinner, because she has no time to cook. She has to study hard.

At 2:00am, Haruna closes her textbook.

She thinks, *I can't do this. I can't get 700. Maybe I should quit my job. I am tired every day. I work very hard, then I come home and study. I have no time to make dinner. I eat cup noodles and other convenience store food. It is not healthy. I have no time to see my friends. I want a new job. Tomorrow, I will look for a new job!*

CHAPTER SIX

It is Saturday afternoon. Haruna is in the bookshop looking at a magazine. The magazine is *Tenshoku Joho Zasshi*. It is a magazine about jobs and careers. She is looking for a new job.

"Excuse me!"

Haruna looks behind her.

There is a tall, thin woman with blonde hair. She is looking at Haruna, and she is speaking in English. Haruna is very surprised.

"Er…yes?" says Haruna, nervously.

"Are there any English books in this bookshop?" asks the woman.

"Er…yes, but….er..." says Haruna. She feels very nervous.

"Yes? Pardon?" says the woman.

"The English books are Japanese books," says Haruna.

"The English books are Japanese books? I don't understand," says the woman.

Haruna cannot explain.

"Please come with me. I will show you," says Haruna.

Haruna and the woman walk to the English book section.

"The English books," says Haruna, pointing to the books. "Japanese."

"Ah, I see! Now I understand! The English books are textbooks for Japanese people learning English!" says the woman. She smiles at Haruna.

"Yes, yes. That's right," says Haruna. She feels excited. The woman understood!

"I'd like to buy some books. Are there any bookstores with English books for native English speakers near here?" asks the woman.

"Er...yes, but..." Haruna stops. She cannot explain in English. "Okay, I will take you to the shop" says Haruna.

"Oh really? Thank you! You are so kind! I'm sorry to trouble you!" says the woman.

"It is no problem," says Haruna. She wants to help the woman.

They walk outside into the busy street.

"I'm Julie. I'm from the USA. Nice to meet you," says the woman.

"I'm Haruna. Nice to meet you too," says Haruna.

"Your English is very good, Haruna," says Julie.

"No, no! My English is very bad!" says Haruna. "But I have to learn English for my job. It is very difficult."

"Oh really? What is your job?"

"I work for Nice Ume-leaf Cosmetics."

"Oh, I love Nice Ume-leaf Cosmetics! But I can only buy the cosmetics in Japan. I can't buy them in the USA," says Julie.

"No, not yet," says Haruna.

"My family and friends in LA really like Nice Ume-leaf Cosmetics, so I always send them some Nice Ume-leaf Cosmetics products – mascara, eye shadow and foundation, for birthdays and Christmas."

"Oh really?" Haruna is surprised.

"Yes. Your cosmetics are wonderful. So, are you studying TOEIC?" asks Julie.

"Yes, but my score was not good...I only got 585," says Haruna.

"585 is a good score!" says Julie. "Well done!"

"But I need 700. If I don't get 700, I will lose my job," says Haruna.

"You will lose your job? That's terrible!" says Julie. "How do you study?"

"I use textbooks. I learn new words every day, but I cannot remember them. I forget them quickly," says Haruna.

"Do you practice speaking? Do you go to an English conversation school?" asks Julie.

"No, I don't. I had a trial lesson at an English conversation school, but...my co-worker was in the same class...and...I don't like my co-worker," says Haruna quietly.

Julie laughs.

"I see! Well, I think you need to practice speaking. Only studying from textbooks is no good. English is a communication tool. You have to practice speaking and using English," says Julie.

"Yes, but…I can't speak English," says Haruna.

"Of course you can!" says Julie. "You are speaking English very well with me now!"

Haruna is surprised. *Oh yes! I am! I am speaking English!* She is very pleased.

Haruna and Julie arrive at the bookstore.

"Here it is," says Haruna. "There are some English books in this bookstore."

"Thank you so much," says Julie. "Oh. Next Saturday at the International Centre, there is an International Chat Party. There will be many people from many countries. Why don't you come to the party? You can practice your English."

"Oh really? What time does it start?" asks Haruna.

"It starts at 6:00pm," says Julie. "Please come!"

"OK, thank you. Maybe I will go to the chat party," says Haruna.

CHAPTER SEVEN

It is Saturday evening. Haruna walks into the International Centre. There are many people at the chat party. She feels nervous. She looks around the room. There are many people from many different countries. She looks for Julie. *Where is Julie?* She cannot see her.

"Yamane san!"

Haruna looks behind her. Oh no! It's Kana!

"Oh, hello Matsumoto san," says Haruna.

"Why are you here?" asks Kana.

"Because I want to practice my English," says Haruna.

"Who told you about this party?" asks Kana.

"My American friend, Julie," says Haruna.

"You have an American friend?" asks Kana. She looks surprised.

"Yes, I do," says Haruna.

"Where is she?" asks Kana.

Haruna looks around the room. Where is Julie?

"Er…she will come later," says Haruna.

"Haruna! Haruna! Hi! Thank you for coming! I am very pleased to see you!"

Haruna looks behind her. She sees Julie.

"Hi Julie!" says Haruna. She is very happy to see Julie.

"Is this your friend?" asks Julie.

"This is my co-worker, Kana Matsumoto," says Haruna.

"Oh, I see. Nice to meet you," says Julie.

"Nice to meet you too," says Kana. "Please excuse me. I have to go to the bathroom," says Kana. She walks away.

"Haruna, come with me," says Julie. "I will introduce you to my friends."

Julie introduces Haruna to her friends. Julie's friends are from France, China, Korea, Italy, Australia, Iran and India. Some of them speak Japanese very well. Everyone speaks English. Haruna enjoys talking with Julie's friends.

At the end of the party, she exchanges email addresses with her new friends.

Haruna goes home. She feels very pleased. She spoke lots of English at the party, and she had a very good time. Also, she made many new friends.

Haruna sits on the sofa in the living room and opens a bottle of red wine. She pours a glass of wine and relaxes. She thinks about studying English.

Every day I study English with textbooks. I try to learn new words, but I forget them easily. I am studying English like a high school student. That is why it is difficult for me! I am only studying English for the test! I should use English more! English is a communication tool! If I speak more English, I will remember more words. Also, speaking with friends is good listening practice. And it is fun! Yes! English is fun! I need English. Of course, I need to get 700 points on the TOEIC test, but I also need English to speak to my new friends. From tomorrow, I will study harder, and I will enjoy emailing and talking with my new friends!

CHAPTER EIGHT

Haruna meets her new friends every weekend. She enjoys eating and drinking with them. Everyone likes Haruna. She is very kind. She tells them about Japan, and she helps them to study Japanese. Also, they tell her about their countries. They try to help Haruna with her TOEIC study. She enjoys listening to their stories, and of course, she enjoys speaking English.

In December, she goes to a Christmas party at Julie's apartment. It is fun. She enjoys cooking Christmas dinner with Julie and her friends. The Christmas food is very delicious. After dinner, they enjoy chatting and watching movies.

At New Year, Haruna usually goes back to Matsue, but this year, she stays in Tokyo and studies English very hard. The TOEIC test is very soon. In the New Year holiday, Julie goes to Haruna's apartment and helps her to study English. Haruna takes Julie to a shrine for hatsumode. Hatsumode means "the first prayers of the new year" in Japanese. They pray that Haruna can get 700 points on the TOEIC test.

It is January 12th. Today is the day of the TOEIC test. Haruna wakes up early and studies a little. On the train, she listens to her English CD.

She arrives at work. Kana is already at work. She is studying English at her desk.

Haruna receives an email on her mobile phone. It is an email from Julie.

---*Good luck in your test Haruna! You can get 700 points! From Julie---*

Haruna smiles. She feels happy and relaxed.

The test starts. Haruna is very surprised. The listening sections are easy! They are easier than the listening sections on the test last July.

Next, she answers the questions in the grammar and reading sections. She is very surprised. These questions are easier, too!

After the test, Haruna receives another email from Julie.

---*Haruna, how was your test?*---

Haruna answers:

---*It was easier than the test in July!*---

Julie answers:

---*No, it wasn't easier. It was the same. But your English is better now! So you felt it was easier!*---

Haruna replies:

---*Thanks to you Julie!*---

CHAPTER NINE

It is the day of the test results. Everyone in the office looks nervous.

"Please come into the meeting room," says Tanaka kacho.

Everyone walks into the meeting room. Takahashi shacho is sitting at the table! He is not smiling. Everyone feels even more nervous. Tanaka kacho also looks nervous.

"I will announce your TOIEC scores. Adachi san – 700, Sato san – 710, Saito san – 700, Matsumoto san – 790, Yamane san – 785," says Tanaka kacho.

Everyone relaxes. They all got over 700! Everyone studied very hard. Haruna got over 700 points. She is happy, but also a little sad. Kana's score is higher. Kana got 790 points. Kana looks at Haruna and smiles.

"I am going to the USA," says Kana quietly.

Haruna does not answer her.

"Everyone tried their best. Well done. Everyone scored over 700 points," says Takahashi shacho. "Yamane san and Matsumoto san, after the meeting, please come to my office. I want to talk to you."

Everyone goes back to the office.

"Congratulations!"

"We all did really well! Let's celebrate tonight! Let's go to a bar! Let's drink!"

Everyone is very happy. They got over 700 points, so they will not lose their jobs.

Haruna and Kana go to Takahashi shacho's office.

Kana knocks on the door.

"Come in!" says Takahashi shacho.

They go into the office and sit down. The office is on the top floor of the building. From the windows, there are wonderful views of Tokyo.

Takahashi shacho smiles at Haruna and Kana.

"Yamane san, Matsumoto san, you both did very well on the TOEIC test. Well done," says Takahashi shacho.

"Thank you," say Haruna and Kana.

"Last year, Tanaka kacho told you that the person with the highest score can go to the USA. Matsumoto san, you have the highest score. Congratulations. You will start working in New York in April."

Kana is very happy. "Thank you Takahashi shacho. I will work very hard in New York. I promise!" she says.

"Congratulations," says Haruna sadly.

Then, Takahashi shacho says, "Two months ago, an American woman came to our shop in Ginza. She said 'I like your cosmetics very much. My friends and family in California love Nice Ume-leaf Cosmetics. I send your cosmetics as birthday and Christmas presents. Many people in LA are waiting for Nice Ume-leaf Cosmetics to open a shop there.' So, I decided to start with two shops in the USA – one in New York, in the east, and one in LA, in the west. Yamane san, would you like to work at the shop in LA?"

Haruna looks very surprised. She cannot speak. She cannot believe it.

"Yamane san? Do you want to work at the shop in LA? Yes? No?" asks Takahashi shacho.

Haruna smiles. "Yes! Yes! Of course yes! Thank you Takahashi shacho! Thank you!"

"Good. Yamane san, you will start working in LA in April," says Takahashi shacho.

Kana looks at Haruna. "Congratulations," she says. But she does not smile.

Haruna goes to the office kitchen and calls Julie on her mobile phone.

"Julie! I got 785 points!" says Haruna.

"Congratulations!" says Julie. "Did you get the highest score?"

"No, my co-worker got the highest score, but the president wants two shops – one in LA and one in New York. He asked me to work in the LA shop!" says Haruna.

"That's great!" says Julie. "Congratulations! My family and friends will be very happy."

"Julie…did you go to the Nice Ume-leaf Cosmetics shop in Ginza two months ago?" asks Haruna?

Julie laughs. "Yes, I did! How do you know?"

Haruna smiles. "Julie, are you free tonight?"

"Yes, I am," says Julie.

"Good. Because I want to buy you a drink to say thank you!" says Haruna.

"Why? I didn't do anything. No, Haruna. I will buy you a drink because you passed your test!" says Julie.

"No, no, Julie. I owe you a drink! Drinks are on me tonight!" says Haruna.

Haruna is very happy, but she is also a little nervous. Will she enjoy life in LA?

Will Nice Ume-leaf Cosmetics become a famous brand in the USA? Will there be any trouble with Kana?

Find out in Haruna's Story Part 2, also available from I Talk You Talk Press.

THANK YOU

Thank you for reading Haruna's Story Part 1! We hope you enjoyed the story. (Word count: 4,820)

There are quizzes about this book on our free study site I Talk You Talk Press EXTRA. http://italk-youtalk.com

If you would like to read more graded readers, please visit our website
http://www.italkyoutalk.com

Other Level 1 graded readers include
A Business Trip to New York
A Homestay in Auckland
A Trip to London
Dear Ellen
Haruna's Story Part 2
Haruna's Story Part 3
Ken's Story Part 1
Ken's Story Part 2
Life is Surprising!
Strange Stories
The Christmas Present
The Old Hospital
We Met Online

ABOUT THE AUTHOR

I Talk You Talk Press is a Japan-based publisher of language textbooks, graded readers and language learning/teaching resources.

Our team is made up of highly experienced language teachers and translators, who have all studied at least one additional language to an advanced level.

This experience enables us to design our materials from the perspective of both the teacher and the learner. We consult with both teachers and language learners when designing our textbooks and graded readers, and test our materials extensively in the classroom before publication.

We are a fast-growing press, and currently publish graded readers for learners of English. We publish new graded readers monthly.